Swallowing the Moon

Swallowing the Moon

by
Alicia Otis

SUNSTONE PRESS

SANTA FE

Book design by Vicki Ahl.
Cover photograph by the author, enhanced by Carl Johansen.
Author photograph by Carl Johansen.
Calligraphy by Fayeq Oweis.

© 2007 by Alicia Otis. All Rights Reserved.
No part of this book may be reproduced in any form or by any electronic or mechanical means including information storage and retrieval systems without permission in writing from the publisher, except by a reviewer who may quote brief passages in a review.

Sunstone books may be purchased for educational, business, or sales promotional use. For information please write: Special Markets Department, Sunstone Press, P.O. Box 2321, Santa Fe, New Mexico 87504-2321.

Library of Congress Cataloging-in-Publication Data

Otis, Alicia, 1934-
  Swallowing the moon : poems / by Alicia Otis.
    p. cm.
  ISBN 0-86534-569-4 (pbk. : alk. paper)
  1. Title.

PS3565.T46S93 2007
811'.54--dc22

                              2006038491

WWW.SUNSTONEPRESS.COM
SUNSTONE PRESS / POST OFFICE BOX 2321 / SANTA FE, NM 87504-2321 / USA
(505) 988-4418 / ORDERS ONLY (800) 243-5644 / FAX (505) 988-1025

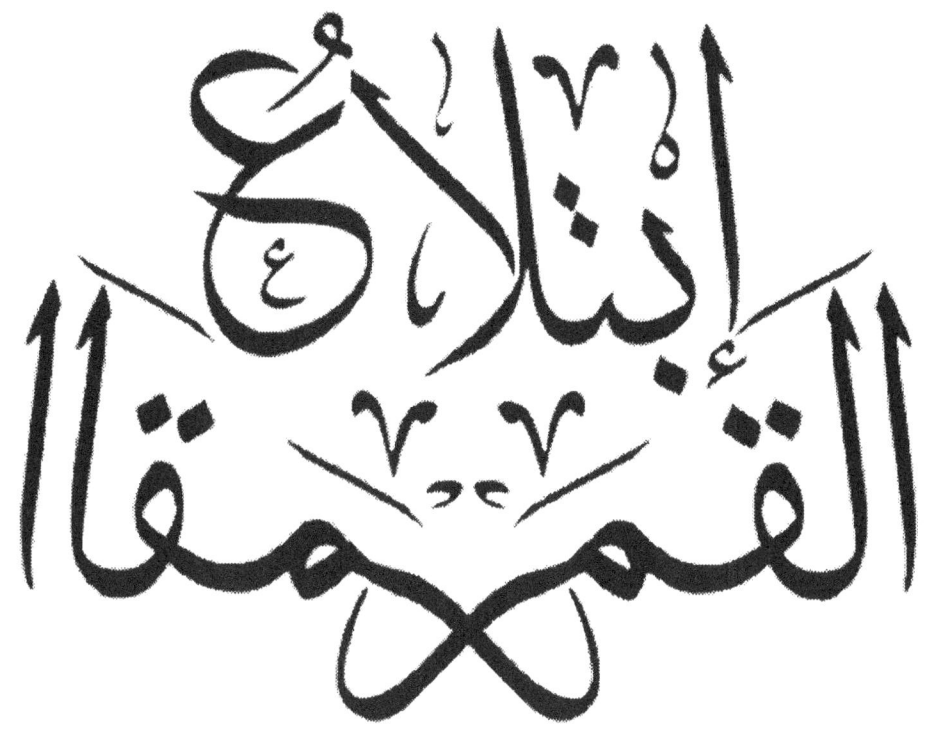

Swallowing the Moon

Calligraphy by Fayeq Oweis

For Maata Lynn Barron

*Love refuses nothing and takes nothing;
It is the highest and vastest freedom*

—Gospel of Phillip

CONTENTS

ACKNOWLEDGMENTS / 13
PREFACE / 15

Sea of Love: A Dialogue / 21
Drowning / 23
Sweet Chariot / 25
Blessed Are They / 27
Empty / 29
Whisper Me to You / 31
Clearing the Slate / 33
Calligraphy Lesson 1 / 35
Tumbleweeds / 37
Untitled / 39
Waking the Birds / 41
In the Distance / 43
Winter Moon / 45
In a Lifetime / 47
Albatross / 49
Leaf and Poppy / 51
Calligraphy Lesson 2 / 53
The Swan / 55

Desert Reds / 57
Calligraphy Lesson 3 / 59
Where the River
Bends North / 61
Wonder of Origin / 63
Those Days / 65
Moon Bird / 67
Bright Waves / 69
Soul Ship / 71
Last Night / 73
Salt / 75
The Camel / 77
The Sweetest Sounds / 79
Empty Seashell / 81
Morning After Returning
Home from Brooklyn / 83
Calling / 85

ACKNOWLEDGMENTS

I am grateful to my teacher, Llewellyn Vaughan Lee, and to my current teacher, Maata Lynn Barron, for tending my heart so lovingly; to my friends, Anne Scott, Linda Kammer, Charlotte Bruce, Elizabeth Peacock, Ethel Fisher, Lisa Kleger; to my friend and writing teacher, Carol Moldaw; to my loyal writing group in Burlingame, California: I thank you all for listening to and reading my poems; for offering your astute suggestions, patience, and encouragement to dig deeper into the heart of each poem to find the hidden treasure waiting to be uncovered. Thanks to Carl Johansen for his technical assistance and for enhancing the photographs.

Special thanks to my dear friend and editor, Nancy Hopkin, in appreciation for our friendship based on a mutual dedication to the Path; to her generosity, loyalty, and love, and to her acute sensibilities, which detected something ringing in my early poems that she thought worthy of exploring together with me. Without her encouragement, I might have drifted off to yet another artistic pursuit.

PREFACE

Writing poetry is one way I express my love and devotion to the Presence of the Unknown She, the Divine Light of the (nongendered) feminine principle of God. For most of my life She was hidden inside of my heart. But now this Light is no longer hidden. It's the illumination of my life, and She has entered the realm of my consciousness. Every morning and night I wake up in Her Presence.

This is not the same light as the sun's. It's the quality of Light that has never been touched by fire. It's the Light (Love) that illuminates the empty, black space in the universe. The same quality of Light is in every particle of dust and every drop of water in the oceans, rivers, ponds, streams, and lakes—it's in the concrete surrounding shopping malls. It's the hidden Light through which Her creation becomes manifest—the Light within the heart of every human being.

She's the Light that IS for those who have eyes that see. Her wisdom IS for those who have ears that hear. In previous times, only the initiated had access to that kind of perception, but now She is present in a new way, available to anyone who sincerely seeks the Truth. One only has to focus one's attention inward and listen. When I listen, She speaks to me in poetry.

I first heard about Maata Lynn Barron five years ago, when I was visiting friends in California. I was told that she had experienced a total annihilation of the small self, or ego. Immediately my heart quickened, and I knew that I had to meet this woman who carries the transmission of the Unknown She. I knew that she was a saint, and that she was someone I had been waiting to meet for as long as I can remember.

I finally met Lynn a year later, when she and another friend gave a day retreat in the living room of a friend's house on the Point Reyes Peninsula. Lynn spoke very little that day. As far as I was concerned, Lynn didn't ever need to speak. The silence that emanated from and around her filled my heart with joy and gladness. I was embodied in Truth. Words would have been a distraction from the immediacy of my experience. This kind of energy impacts the heart, not the mind. From Heart to Heart, It moves faster than the speed of light.

Several more years passed. I took the opportunity to sit with Lynn once or twice during that time, whenever I could. Then she and another friend came to Taos, New Mexico, during the summer to give a three-day retreat. At that time Lynn discovered that I wrote poetry, and she asked me to sit in front of the group that evening and read some of my poems. Lynn was using me to make a point, to me and to everyone else attending the retreat, that most of us are further along in our spiritual unfoldment than we realize.

The moment I started reading my poem, I felt the power of the transmission go through my body. I was filled with Light. Someone's voice (mine, of course) was reading the words of my poem. I heard the sound echoing from the back of the darkened room. I was dimly aware that I was the reader, but at the same time, whoever "I" had become felt completely detached from the reader.

From that moment on, writing devotional poetry to the Unknown She became my spiritual practice. I get up at four AM and meditate until a little after dawn. Then, for the next three hours, I wait in front of my computer screen for poems to emerge. Sometimes words appear in a poem that come not from me, but from a hidden resource inside my heart.

Through this practice I experience Her Presence unfolding wisdom inside of me. Slowly I am becoming aware of who She is, of Her attributes of beauty, goodness, and wisdom. In me She lives predominantly as Joy and Peace; sometimes Her sweetness enters my heart.

I am an ordinary person, perhaps like you, who always longed for something that seemed to be always just beyond my reach. I waited for sixty-five years before I discovered the Source of my longing. It wasn't another relationship, or recognition as an artist; it wasn't a journey to a foreign country or living in exotic Hawaii, or (although this is a source of great pleasure) watching my grandchildren grow up.

What I longed to experience—not in the abstract, intellectual way, but as a visceral, organic, experience of the REAL—was the Treasure of Divine Light/Love, longing to be unveiled and made conscious in the hearts and minds of all human beings. And I wanted to be able to connect with other people through their Light, whether it was veiled or awakened. Nobody is completely asleep. Love, our true nature, reveals our hidden Self to us in the most surprising ways.

On earth things are never as they appear. Once we awaken to Her Light, we see with our eyes that see how suffering, sorrow, disillusion, despair, and separation are veils that we project upon the Divine Reality of Love within ourselves. This unconscious distortion of Reality reflects the same collective anti-life illusions upon others, our living planet, and all creatures upon it.

Her Presence inside each one of us, made conscious by an act of Grace, transforms the illusions and distortions into peace, gnosis-wisdom-Light, that Reality which is Love, the root of our origin. These poems are my way of bearing witness to that transformational Presence of the Unknown She alive in all of us.

Seen and unseen
Love moves eternity in
And down through us
As consciousness unfolds
Herself to Herself, darkly
And lightly—
Light upon Light

Mysterious One,
Light the world with your Luminous Face
The hidden Face we are becoming—
Same as our enemies' Faces
Unfold through time,
The way we looked
Before we were born

—Alicia Otis
Santa Fe, New Mexico

Sea of Love

A Dialogue

*Extraordinary mind
Look where you have taken me—
This albatross of words
Flying around and around,
Across and above the Sea—*

Drop me. I'm wordless, naked,
Ready to drown in the Sea of Love.

*Whose warrior heart
Is that still circling
Up so high?*

It's mine.

Where is the stone
That will take me down?

Swallow the moon

Drowning

I called to the mockingbird
Sitting in her tree:

"I'm drowning
In this Sea of Love"

She added drowning
To her repertoire of borrowed calls:
Sparrow, finch, bluebird,
Wind chimes and farting motorcycles

Lark sparrow
Sings from her nest
In the reeds by the lily pond:

*Spring, drowning,
Water, sky*

Mockingbird,
By heart, whose song
Knows you best?

*Reed flute
Cut from her reed bed,
Crying—Hu*

⏺   HU: In Arabic, the genderless pronoun of Divine Presence. Repeated in a chant, *Hu* is a love song to the Beloved.

Sweet Chariot

A day doesn't slip by
Without a new or an old song
Reminding me of You.

If I don't hum Swing Low,
Lovesick Blues, Wade in the Water
Or new variations of these themes
Longing gangs up on me
And pounds my heart
As if it were a closed door
Until I wake up, listen and open.

Blessed Are They

Light—
Not from lightning
But from the hoof of the she-camel
Striking First Rock
In the desert

Out flew water
Cool and salted—

Love was this
Before darkness arrived—

Before suns and swallowing moons

Before She became earth

Before time flew out of His eye

Before mothers and fathers
Made daughters and sons—

And the storm that followed

Worship with tears
What you don't understand

Love His design—
Be Her fire—

Ignite this stream of life
With your Light torch kiss

Blessed are they
Who breathe earth in
And come back empty

Empty

I gave Her everything I have to give—
My heart, my daughter, this sky of skies—

When I walk beneath blue blue emptiness
Oh Love, it's never empty enough—

The distance between You and me,
That blessed grief for which we are comforted
Rolls on—

Deserts are thirsty places—
These waterless clouds—

Mine, the thirst of the mourning dove

Dark is day

Joy-Light in the night
Neither sun, nor moon, nor star—

Light from no candle lit,

Everything is Light

Whisper Me to You

She fills the room like a garment

For a moment, I wear Her empty space; the fireplace,
Lively candle flame

Outside, cool morning breeze, rain clouds—
Peace She is—

This love song has no beginning
No end

Whisper me between the lines—
Whisper me to You

Wind blows through Her grass a cappella

Many beings; grass, dog, candle flame
All of us: One

Go into silence as One

Love plucks us from Her breast
Bountiful seeds of Light,
We fall to Her earth,
Most of us stay.
We wrestle with light and darkness.
Dance if you can.

Some are lost. She forgives,
Begins again.

Whisper me between the lines—
Whisper me to You

Clearing the Slate

I'm clearing my slate
So that She finds me clean—
Empty as the morning sky

No thought or concept
Mars the beauty of Her Face

Gone, my precious ideals like jeweled gowns
Hung side by side in a queen-size closet,
Each skin fit like shimmering eel

People seeing me walk into a room
Would say: How lovely—

Now the closet is empty.
Naked, lying on the floor
I watch four walls and ceiling fade away.
Night enters the room.

Something marks the slate.

Inside my heart
Emptiness,
Free of itself

Calligraphy Lesson 1

Put down your brush.

Watch Her paint your poem about rocks
After the rain leaves them shining

Ask Her to teach you from emptiness
About lines with no edges.

Watch your beautiful words disappear
Emerging as stones
Smoothed in Her Sea.

The painter/poet you were—
Watch her drown in Her pot of black ink.

Now you're the one you longed to be
Vanished inside the rock
Listening to Love's heartbeat
Tap the way Love rolls
Underneath the sea

Tumbleweeds

Two times I woke to the sound of waves
Slapping the sides of my fishing skiff
Drifting down Love River

Later, I knew those sounds
Were just the wind
Rattling the shutters of my desert house

Come!
Let's take a walk in the open land
Where distance has no end
And weeds the size of fishing skiffs
Tumble across red dust

Untitled

I watched Her pass through emptiness
I saw the threads of night blowing around Her feet

She glides along an invisible strand
Stretched across a drift beyond my imagination

Her balance pole
Some long flexible fiber
A point of light blazing each tip
Swizzles through gray mist

Waking the Birds

The place in your heart
Where your Beloved resides
Softly, sweetly

Abide there
Awake asleep

Naked as the morning sky
Joined with your Beloved
Blessings pour forth
To all you meet

Your beam of light
Touches Earth
Penetrates the sea

Divine you are—humanly so
She/He loves us for that

Speak not.
Wait and listen.
The tide is turning inward
Where your Beloved resides
Where you abide

Awake/asleep
Listening—not for words
But for the wave of glory
Waking birds in the field
Where you live

In the Distance

In the distance
I see Her emptiness

Close by
Her hand takes mine—
We dance

Winter Moon

Winter.
Moonlight dancing on the ceiling—

Soon it will be gone—

Cling to nothing
Especially love

When the ceiling's empty,
Mysterious mistress soul,
Who will dance with you?

Darkness, darkness
Virgin night,
Come down

This bed is cold
Without you

In a Lifetime

In a lifetime
Of willful, anti-love pursuits,
Even though I didn't know Her then
A part of me always drifted
Beside Her

He nudged me
Down my trail of broken hearts
Until the morning came
When His fist,
Clutching a bunch of wild violets,
Burst out of a turbulent cloud—

Part of me said Yes to Him
But it wasn't until later
When I dropped into Her Heavenly Sea—

Where the luminous part of me
Drifts beside the luminous part of You—

That Love turned me into a lover

Albatross

Oh silent One
My day fell apart—
This day is Yours.

Actually, all days are Yours
But when dark clouds roll in
I lose sight of my anchor of Light

As if an albatross
Had flown between us
Snipped the rope

Where am I then?

That's when I run to my boat
Clip the mooring line,
Ride the riptide out to sea
Then pray for the wind to take me

Leaf and Poppy

Even if I could capture
A sunny day's sheer river rapture
It would be a skewed reflection
Of emptiness—

Leaf rushing by
I long to be like you
Taken by currents
Beyond your control

Poppies' roots
Firm their place on earth—
All they can do is open to the sun—
When the light goes down
Their petals enclose them

Thus begins night's
Long dream of Light

Calligraphy Lesson 2

Where Her love line
Curves in
A little to the east
She takes my western brush
Dips it in the pot of indigo black

Paper spins

Line sweeps north
Aurora borealis
Arctic moon

No mind

Just tides of vital breath,
Ignited dust,
The brush I can't imagine
Dips into a sea of midnight ink—
She paints Herself, the Origin of Light

The Swan

About the swan you see across the lake
Whiteness veiled in morning mist
Parting the waters behind her

Purity undaunted by ripples or waves

Do you tremble at her beauty?
Does your heart flutter,
Young man in love,
Seeing this hidden part of yourself
Gliding across the lake?

My love, she is who she is,
But she's not Light from the beyond

Hold her if you can
Smooth her feathers,
Stroke her long bowed neck,
But don't confuse this beauty
With Hers

Desert Reds

Night
In the ocean
We wear luminous black.
Our lungs become gills

We live inside seashells
With mollusks and crabs

We move in slow motion

Dawn
We return to the land
Wearing green mixed with rocks
And desert reds—

We breathe air,
Open our eyes and hearts to the sun
All day we follow light across the sky.

Twilight
We hang green on rocks and trees,
Rush into the sea
And drown

Calligraphy Lesson 3

Let Her paint you through the moon
Deep into Her darkness

With your cursive brush
Follow the inner line
Where form meets emptiness—

Where you meet the luminous curve—
Her face, Her nose and lips
Lift the brush

Delve into that sweetness

Paint nothing where silence rests

Where the River Bends North

Have you seen Her Light—
Joy notes planted inside your heart?

Have you seen Her house,
Rain cascading off the roof,
No rain clouds in sight?

Tell your friend:
"Follow the river down through Canyon de Chelly"

Still, many are afraid to leave one world
For another—

Patterns of light dance the waves closing in
overhead—

Above the pool where the river bends north
Stands a tall willow
Whose branches etch light trails on the water
So Night can see the miracle revealing
Her Presence.

Wonder of Origin

When dry riverbeds
Give way to flash floods
Dismantling their river banks,
Uprooting rocks, salt cedar shrubs,
Old tires, junk cars, bird skeletons—
All the things you thought you were
Swept away—

So easy to mistake that
Torrent for something
Other than Love returning you empty
To the wonder of your Origin

Those Days

Those days
When Your Light
Beams out from behind my eyes
I wonder if people
Standing in line across from me
At the grocery store
See You and me
Or just You?

Moon Bird

She walked into the desert
Shirt, pants, jacket
Sliding off her skin

Naked
Standing before the moon

No name

She left this world
Singing her sea song,
Every bird in the county
Joined in—

Now she's back,
Surrounded by her horse
Her dog, her sheep and goat,

Singing her sea song

Bright Waves

Beloved,
These seeds You drop in my hair—

Ripening at night
Oh, the flights they take
Between the worlds;
Unseen and Seen

Waking at dawn
I watch waves roll in
Standing up straight
Slight curl at the tip

Waves bright
With Her Light
Lick rocks,
Carpet beaches, gleaming
Before ironed sand absorbs them—

One wave followed by another
Then another

Soul Ship

Do you know the ship
Your Soul sails on?

I saw mine one evening—
A long boat cloud
Outer edges of her sails
Trimmed rose-pink

Whatever form she assumes
Your heart will recognize her—

You've been together
Almost forever

Some Souls appear in dreams
Many lose their direction
A few sail straight for the Light

Souls light candles
That sputter and go out as they pass
On their journey to the Unknown

Bright sparrow
Fly through the window

We *are* our Souls
Except for a grain of salt
Savoring Earth's dream

Last Night

Last night

When I woke up

She was calling from the field

Shimmering inside Her cricket gown

I lay in bed

Half moon spinning the sky—

Crick Crick Crick

Salt

Ye are the salt of the earth but if salt loses its flavor wherewith shall it be salted? It is therefore good for nothing but to be cast out and trodden underfoot of man.
—The Beatitudes

She slips in through night
Between the winds of Glory and Hallelujah

I chain my mind to the mast. Open the sail
Until She's running free before the wind
Salt spray stinging my skin—

Hand on the tiller neither yours or mine

Her salt flavors wisdom's bright wind
Savor wisdom on your tongue—
Taste it and remember—
You are Earth's salt

Forgetting that
What are you good for?

Earth endures, sucking in her womb,
Her breasts and belly

Humming, Earth waits
For her wisdom people to brighten and rise
Like bread in the oven

The Camel

The camel sits down
She won't budge
If you're carrying baggage
If you're wearing clothes

Sometimes,
Ready or not,
She takes you—sweet mystery,
Pregnant with Love,
Ripe for falling
Stranded on earth
Performing acts of love,
Remembering and forgetting
To tend every weed and flower along the path
As if it were the first and the last

The Sweetest Sounds

Beloved—
I am one who hears Your sweetest sounds:
Shaah, rhee, maah, su—Hu

Mists at the ends of words
Sung by those—children, women,
Men, birds—
Who love only You

Empty Seashell

This morning
She's the sea coming in

Yesterday green wrapped around Her

Tomorrow I may not be here
Having dropped inside Her

Sea turtles
Wind—

When I thought of the moon
She whispered, *Hu*

I miss "me" a little;
Beachcomber
Runner, grandmother, artist

I was not all that different
From this empty seashell
Who tried to paint Wind
And failed.

Morning After Returning Home from Brooklyn

Without Her Light inside my chest
Earth, where would you have been?

Who would have heard the moon splash down
And seen her push Li Po off his riverboat of longing?

When the mourning doves call *Remember, Hu Hu Hu*
You'd better slip through the window before
    moonstruck water
Pulls you in.

Calling

Someone's calling—
Or is it the sound of Light
Filling Her sail?

The boat left without me

Shorelines tremble
Each time She leaves
A nomad behind

Is that sound of longing
My voice—

Or is it some wind
Swallowing the moon?

This book of poetry has been printed on acid-free paper.

The typeface is Futura Lt BT.

Futura, first presented by the Bauer Type Foundry in 1928, is commonly considered the major typeface development to come out of the Constructivist orientation of the Bauhaus.movement in Germany. Paul Renner (type designer, painter, author and teacher) sketched the original drawings and based them loosely on the simple forms of circle, triangle and square. Futura is timelessly modern; in 1928 it was striking, tasteful, radical— and today it continues to be a popular typographic choice to express strength, elegance, and conceptual clarity.

www.ingramcontent.com/pod-product-compliance
Lightning Source LLC
Chambersburg PA
CBHW021022090426
42738CB00007B/870